I'LL BE THERE FOR YOU

FOR YOU

LIFE ACCORDING TO FRIENDS'

RACHEL,

PHOEBE,

JOEY,

CHANDLER,

ROSS & **MONICA**

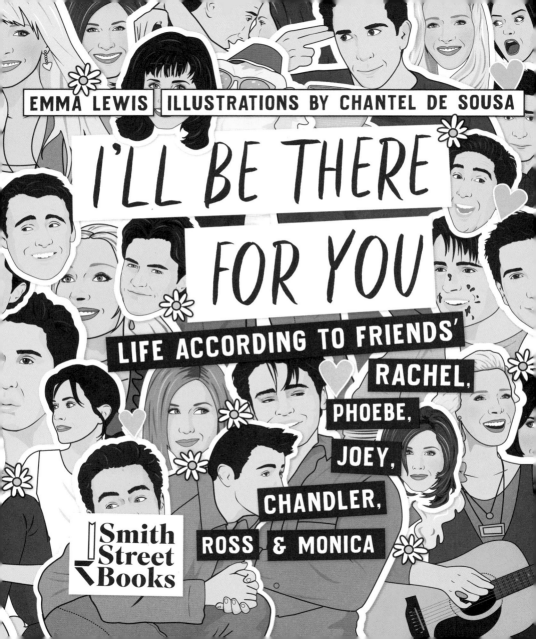

EMMA LEWIS ILLUSTRATIONS BY CHANTEL DE SOUSA

I'LL BE THERE FOR YOU

LIFE ACCORDING TO FRIENDS' RACHEL, PHOEBE, JOEY, CHANDLER, ROSS & MONICA

Smith Street Books

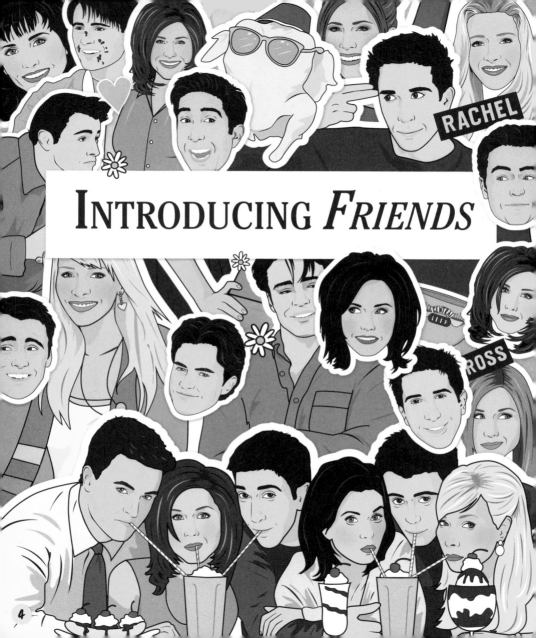

INTRODUCING *FRIENDS*

RACHEL

ROSS

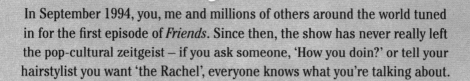

In September 1994, you, me and millions of others around the world tuned in for the first episode of *Friends*. Since then, the show has never really left the pop-cultural zeitgeist – if you ask someone, 'How you doin?' or tell your hairstylist you want 'the Rachel', everyone knows what you're talking about.

Audiences were immediately drawn to *Friends*, and by season two, it was a worldwide phenomenon. It was a pleasure to follow the six friends' adventures as twenty-somethings becoming thirty-somethings, particularly for those of us who were around the same age at the time. Many of us related to the characters' highs and lows in love, at work and at home, and admit it – we all wish that we lived in New York City in an apartment that was impossibly large relative to our paygrade.

It isn't hard to see a little of ourselves in each of the friends. We've all felt like a Ross when he had his spectacular meltdown at work over a stolen sandwich, and we've all felt like a Rachel when she struggled to make rent on her sad Central Perk pay cheque. And speaking of Ross and Rachel, every person in the universe can be divided into two groups depending on whether or not they think Ross and Rachel were really 'on a break' or not.

There were countless hilarious moments in *Friends*, but also some truly touching ones. We all felt Phoebe's pain when she gave up the triplets, and our hearts ached for Monica and Chandler when they found out they couldn't conceive a child. *Friends* had the perfect sitcom balance of hilarity and heart, and remained popular throughout its entire ten-year run.

Even though *Friends* left our screens way back in 2004, audiences worldwide still religiously watch reruns, and any rumour of a reunion is met with unbridled glee. The six stars have gone on to enjoy successful acting careers, but we'll always know them best as Monica, Rachel, Phoebe, Ross, Joey and Chandler.

So for those of you looking for a little more from your favourite friends, I present *I'll Be There for You*.

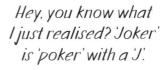
Hey, you know what I just realised? 'Joker' is 'poker' with a 'J'.

Coincidence?

Hey, that's 'joincidence' with a 'C'.

WHICH FRIEND

ARE YOU?

Do you identify as a Monica, but harbour a secret inner Phoebe?
Are you a Chandler on the streets but a Joey in the sheets?
Were you on a break like Ross, or definitely *not* on a break like Rachel?
Want to know which Friend you are once and for all? Take this easy quiz!

1. DESCRIBE YOUR BIGGEST-EVER FASHION SPLURGE.

a. Expensive knee-high boots so uncomfortable that I momentarily had no feeling from the waist down.
b. A purse worth more than the average college fund (but I used my staff discount so it was basically free, right?).
c. Leather pants that I would rather not discuss, thank you.
d. Ferrari jacket with matching hat and keyring. A huge mistake.
e. 100% mohair sweater vest. And I still have it.
f. A purple crushed-velvet dress to show off my assets in a classy and definitely non-slutty manner.

2. WHAT WAS YOUR LAST REASON FOR CALLING IN SICK?

a. I would never call in sick! I love my job. Calling in sick is for quitters.
b. A smudged pedicure.
c. Too devastated to get out of bed after a paper was rejected by *Nature*.
d. My date with twins ran into the next business day.
e. The crushing realisation that I am a corporate shill.
f. A haunted wardrobe.

3. DESCRIBE YOUR FAVOURITE MEAL.

a. Thanksgiving with all the trimmings.
b. Sushi at my desk.
c. Thanksgiving turkey sandwich prepared by Monica.
d. All sandwiches in general.
e. Officially, T-bone steak. Unofficially, Crêpes Suzette.
f. Vegan bacon and eggs.

4. DESCRIBE YOUR HAIRSTYLE IN ONE WORD.

a. Practical (unless there's any humidity involved).
b. Perfection.
c. Bouffant.
d. Inconsequential – my face is a masterpiece.
e. Flippy-floppy.
f. Breezy.

5. WHAT'S YOUR FAVOURITE MUSICAL?

a. *Mary Poppins*, particularly the songs that describe tidying.
b. *Hair*.
c. Officially, *Miss Saigon*. Unofficially, *Wicked*.
d. Does *Die Hard* have a soundtrack?
e. *Annie*, 1982 cast.
f. How could you ask me this? I hardly got to see any musicals when I GREW UP ON THE STREETS.

6. DESCRIBE YOUR ULTIMATE NIGHT OUT.

a. Cooking for eight.
b. Shopping for eight.
c. The planetarium.
d. Two dates.
e. Beating my record on *Pac-Man*.
f. Ice skating or target shooting, preferably both at the same time.

7. WHAT LITTLE THING DO YOU DO TO SAVE THE ENVIRONMENT?

a. Only using natural cleaning products (unless I'm cleaning the bathroom, kitchen or any other surface I actually touch with my bare hands).
b. Giving up all beauty treatments that contain plastic microbeads.
c. Arguing to anyone who will listen that climate change is scientific fact like the air we breathe, like gravity.
d. Using only 100% natural latex condoms.
e. Recycling all of my jokes.
f. Composting my own hair.

9. WHAT IS YOUR FAVOURITE MAGAZINE?

a. *American Grout Inspectors Annual.*
b. *Vogue.*
c. It's a dead heat between *Palaeontology Monthly* and *Palaeobotany Weekly.*
d. *Playboy.*
e. *MAD* magazine.
f. *Rat Fanciers Roundtable.*

8. WHAT IS YOUR SIGNATURE COCKTAIL?

a. Vodka neat – it doubles as a stain remover for delicate fabrics.
b. Vodka, lime and soda – 70 calories, gets the job done.
c. Funky Monkey.
d. Sex on the Beach.
e. Officially, Whiskey Sour. Secretly, Mint Julep.
f. Vegan Bloody Mary with facon.

10. WHAT ARE YOU MOST PROUD OF?

a. Getting everyone at work to adhere to my strict hand-washing program.
b. My handbag collection.
c. Making tenure.
d. Beating my own record for jars of jam consumed in an evening.
e. Getting the high score on *Space Invaders* at the arcade near my house in 1984.
f. My collection of living hats.

MOSTLY A?

YOU ARE MONICA

You are organised, competitive and a bit of a neat freak.
You are sensible but scrappy, and your friends know they can rely
on you for anything. No challenge is too small and you are always
playing to win. You once stayed awake all night fantasising about
cleaning the ceiling fan at work, then went in at 4 am to do it.

MOSTLY B?

YOU ARE RACHEL

You are fun, stylish and always on-trend. You sicken your friends with your ability to look beautiful in sweatpants and a dirty T-shirt. You either work in fashion or simply set the trends by walking down the street. You once had a friend hold you by the ankles while you fished for a new shoe that you accidentally kicked into the Hudson River.

MOSTLY C?

YOU ARE ROSS

You are smart, slightly shy and maybe just a little unlucky in love.
You follow your dreams and work hard on your passions, despite
the fact that nobody has any idea what you are talking about. You once
stayed awake for fifty hours to complete an important piece of work and
apologised to a shopping bag full of pineapples on the subway after
falling asleep on them. The texture of your hair is inexplicable.

MOSTLY D?

YOU ARE JOEY

You are lovable, flirty and have dated more people than
Warren Beatty. You probably get away with more than you should
because you are so damn charming. You are most likely employed in
a creative field, or wish that you were. Your 'magic number' requires
an exponentiation to fit on a calculator screen.

MOSTLY E?

YOU ARE CHANDLER

You're funny, charming, and maybe just a little dysfunctional.
You are funnier than Jerry Lewis, but work in a cubicle analysing
data you neither understand nor care about. Smoking is your secret
shame and you are not above eating food off the floor if required.
You once hid behind a potted plant to avoid speaking with a
colleague while waiting for a lift.

MOSTLY F?

YOU ARE PHOEBE

You are an off-beat character who refuses to conform. You are kind and friendly to everyone you meet, even if you've just read their aura and it's clear that they were evil in a previous life. You have never held down a nine-to-five job and don't drink coffee because you never have to be anywhere early in the day. Your lucky colour is the number three.

23

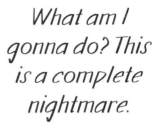

What am I gonna do? This is a complete nightmare.

I know. This must be so hard. 'Oh, no. Two women love me. They're both gorgeous, my wallet's too small for my 50s, and my diamond shoes are too tight.'

HOW YOU DOIN'?

JOEY TRIBBIANI ON DATING IN
THE MODERN WORLD

Everybody knows Joey Tribbiani has a PhD in dating. Joey never sits at home on a Friday night waiting for a text – Joey makes it happen! It's time to stop aimlessly swiping through your dating apps and messaging losers. To really get yourself in the game, check out Joey's smooth moves.

GETTING THE DATE

While I've never had much of a problem with getting dates, I hear that some people can't instantly attract a potential partner by simply making eye contact with them across a crowded subway car. I honestly think the easiest way to attract someone is with a smile and some light-hearted conversation. Not sure what to talk about? My rule is to keep it casual and to steer clear of anything too topical. You don't want to end up in a political argument, so maybe just stick to what you know, like your most cherished sandwich fillings.

PRE-DATE PREPARATION

It goes without saying that a bit of self-care before your date goes a long way. Clean clothes and a shower are important, but a few little finishing touches will really seal the deal. Lift any outfit with a great jacket slung over your shoulder, and don't forget a dab of aftershave just before leaving the house. Not too much though – go too far and you'll end up smelling like a discount-mall perfume warehouse on a hot day.

LOCATION

The location of my dates usually depends on how much money Chandler is willing to lend me. If money is tight and Chandler isn't around, a long romantic walk through the park is a great option. If the weather doesn't suit, choose a romantic movie, but let your date choose which one. Sure – you might end up having to compete for her attention with a member of the Hemsworth family, but it's better than finding your date asleep in her seat after sitting through three hours of *Fast & Furious 9*. If money is no object, I always suggest a great restaurant. Which brings me to the most important consideration of all ...

THE RULES OF DINING

If you've decided to splash out on a restaurant, there are a few things to consider. For obvious reasons, try to choose somewhere with food that isn't too rich or too spicy – when you get home you want to be dealing with unbridled passion, not the unbridled aftermath of a Tex–Mex disaster. Dining out also gives you a chance to put your best manners on show. It goes without saying that you should be kind to your waiter and always leave a generous tip – nobody likes a stingy date!

BRINGING YOUR DATE BACK HOME

The only thing I love more than food is active and open consent! Keep the mood flirty and light-hearted, and keep those lines of communication open. When it's clear that your date wants to take things back to your apartment (or theirs), consider yourself lucky and behave with the utmost respect. Related: it's never polite to unhook a bra until the apartment door is fully closed.

THE BIG REVEAL

HOW RACHEL ROCKS THAT 90S LOOK!

Rachel Green was nothing short of a 90s fashion icon. From her super-stylish wardrobe to her iconic hairstyle that led to millions of women worldwide asking for 'the Rachel', her influence on fashion cannot be understated. Here's Rachel on perfecting her classic 90s look.

HAIR

Great 90s hair is all about avoiding the mistakes many of us made back then (did somebody say 'tightest possible spiral perm on naturally straight hair'?). Volume is important, and can easily be achieved with a good layered cut and body-boosting products like dry shampoo, a modern miracle I wish I'd known about back then.

CLOTHES

I love nothing more than a crisp white shirt that can be dressed up or down depending on occasion. Pair your shirt with blue jeans and a V-neck sweater for a classic casual look. For a more formal look, pair your shirt with a black leather skirt and some killer heels.

SHOES

I'm a huge proponent of the classic 90s look of a super short skirt with long boots. I like to pair a grey or plaid short skirt with knee-length boots in black or a neutral tone. The height of the heel is up to you, but remember to take into consideration how long you'll be on your feet when you wear them. Blisters weren't cool in the 90s, and they certainly aren't now!

MAKEUP

I like to keep my makeup pretty low-key. Less is more when choosing a base, and I like a natural blush with a little bronzer to keep a sun-kissed look during the warmer months. While a matte colour defined the 1990s lip, I usually choose a neutral colour, or just add a little lip gloss before leaving the house. I try not to repeat any of the main 90s makeup sins – like super-thick mascara, extremely thin eyebrows, and lip liner two shades darker than your lipstick!

ACCESSORIES

I tend not to wear too many accessories, and when I do, I keep it minimal and classic. Think diamond-stud earrings, a simple silver bracelet and an elegant designer watch. In winter, I love to add a splash of flair to my outfits with a luxurious scarf or pashmina.

PUTTING IT ALL TOGETHER

There you have it! Stand tall and walk with confidence – you'll be a 90s style icon before you know it!.

LOOKING FOR A NEW CAREER?

DRILL DOWN INTO ROSS' PEER-REVIEWED
ANALYSIS OF GETTING THE JOB YOU WANT

They say that if you love your job, you'll never work a day in your life. This is so true for Ross, who followed his childhood dream to become a palaeontologist. If you want to follow your dreams but don't know where to start, take Ross' career advice below – just be sure to ignore any tips he gives you on getting married …

CHOOSE SOMETHING YOU LOVE AND STICK WITH IT

I knew I wanted to be a palaeontologist specialising in Cretaceous theropods from a very young age – I mean, who wouldn't? For those of you who aren't lucky enough to have found your calling so early, simply think of something you enjoy doing and just go for it. You don't have to be good at it – 10,000 hours of study should suffice and you'll be an expert in no time. Easy!

STUDY HARD

I used to spend long days and even longer nights in the laboratory ensuring my graduate research project ran smoothly. If that meant staying awake for 52 hours straight taking electron micrographs of fossil seeds, then so be it. My professor used to beg me to go home and get some rest, though that might have had something to do with me wearing the same outfit for said 52 hours. I took her advice and got five hours sleep before returning to those seeds because who could resist – am I right?

YOUR FIRST JOB

So you've put in all that effort and finished your dissertation. Even though your studies may have been focused on a niche area of research, it's important not to limit yourself to just one area – your skills are totally transferable. For example, if your graduate research was on conifer evolution in the late Palaeozoic era, you should still apply for the vast array of jobs on offer related to conifer evolution during the early Mesozoic era. There's a world of opportunity out there, so don't restrict yourself to just one era of gymnosperm evolution, silly!

COLLEGE LIFE

College can be such an exciting time, both academically and socially. While it's important to get the balance right, resist the temptation to party too hard. For a popular guy like me who loves to get down and par-tay, I often found myself missing out on events to ensure I had enough rest to get my study done the following day. Only being invited to three parties during my entire time at college helped with this.

GETTING THAT PROMOTION

After a few years working, you'll be looking to get promoted – or in my case, looking to get tenure. This is a huge step and finally offers career stability. To get a promotion like this, you're going to need to 'bring it' and really start to deliver results for your organisation. It wasn't easy, but the year I spent 300 days in a row painstakingly photographing and re-cataloguing 9300 individual fossilised dinosaur remains really sealed the deal for my tenure. The crying and begging might have helped too.

I remember the day I got my first pay cheque, there was a cave-in in one of the mines.

Phoebe, you worked in a mine?

32

No, I worked in a Dairy Queen.

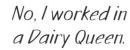

MAKING MUSIC

WITH PHOEBE BUFFET

Phoebe was the musical Friend, always there to entertain us with her unique brand of songwriting and even more unique brand of guitar playing. If you'd like to break into the music scene, tune in to planet Phoebe for some cosmic advice on unleashing your inner chanteuse.

WHAT YOU'LL NEED TO GET STARTED

A guitar. Okay, this one seems obvious, but every project has a starting point, and for learning guitar, this will usually involve having access to a guitar. I was given my first guitar on the streets by a woman who claimed to be a reincarnation of Django Reinhardt, but that doesn't matter. If you end up never running into that lady, a cheap guitar from a second-hand store with some new strings will do.

A can-do attitude. First I ask that you free your mind. You really have to relax before picking up the guitar to let that creativity flow. You need to believe that you can do this. You also need to know that if a word doesn't exist, you can probably just make it up and nobody will notice, especially if it rhymes with the previous line.

Great lyrics. Only sing about what you know. Try to draw on your own personal life experience. For me, other than growing up on the streets and giving birth to my own brother's triplets, my life has been pretty uneventful. For this reason, I like to draw on the experiences of other people for my lyrics. Of course it helps to have a few train wrecks in your life... you wouldn't believe how much mileage I've gotten out of Ross' love life alone!

WHAT YOU SHOULDN'T BOTHER WITH

Lessons. You don't need lessons! Lessons are expensive, and then you're at the mercy of your teacher. This isn't about someone else's style, this is about you! There's nothing I could have learned from a teacher that I didn't learn while straining to hear my grandmother's records over the sound of my mother's tears.

Chord books. Do not get me started on chords. Do not learn them! Just put your fingers where it feels right. 'Bear claw', 'tricky leg' and 'old lady' are a great starting point for any song – maybe throw in a little 'turkey leg' towards the end.

A record contract. If you take my advice, you will need to prepare for the inevitability of fame. Firstly, never sell out to The Man by accepting a record contract. A record contract will stifle your creativity, or worse, make you feel as if you no longer need to busk in the subway all day long for quarters just to make rent. In my opinion, you're better off working for chump change than being at the mercy of a record executive who keeps throwing money at you like the sell-out you've become.

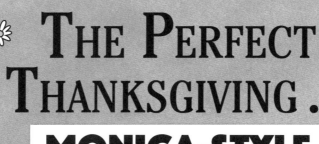

THE PERFECT THANKSGIVING ...

MONICA-STYLE

Monica Geller is famous for her Thanksgiving dinners. No detail is too small to be attended to, with every element down to the napkin-folding as highly choreographed as a Cirque du Soleil show. So come on in, take a seat – NOT THAT ONE! THE OTHER SEAT! – and enjoy a relaxing Thanksgiving, Monica-style.

BEFORE GUESTS ARRIVE

For me, this is the best part, and I can really stretch it out over a number of weeks if I'm organised. Because I pretty much start each day with a blank slate of extreme cleanliness, preparation for Thanksgiving allows me to really concentrate on the little details that make my home special. For example, I go all out to make the bathroom 'just so' for my guests. In the lead-up to Thanksgiving I like to have my fancy guest hand-towels expertly dry cleaned, and I always set aside time to individually hand-carve my guest soaps into festive designs. Even if my guests don't notice the little things, *I* notice, and that's the main thing.

GUESTS WHO WANT TO BRING FOOD

Oh no, that simply won't do. Why stress everyone out with preparing food to my exact specifications? We all remember what happened when Rachel tried to make dessert one year. Thanks, but it's best if I just do it.

DRINKS

Often a guest enjoys being put in charge of the drinks to make them feel special. Personally, I do not have time for that, so I just take care of it. It's simple, really – just plan for any possible cocktail contingency and always have the appropriate glass on hand to serve it in. Then just provide bespoke drink service to each of your guests while still following the Thanksgiving project plan. Too easy!

MEAL PLANNING

As a chef, cooking Thanksgiving dinner is my absolute pleasure. But even if you're not a chef, cooking can still be fun! Speaking of fun, remember to write a detailed project plan to manage the three days before dinner is served. Don't go overboard though – I find dividing the 72-hour period into 432 individual ten-minute blocks stops me from getting stressed out. I prefer not to sleep in the lead-up to Thanksgiving, but you should probably allow yourself three to four hours of sleep per night in your project plan.

ENTERTAINMENT

Guests are usually entertained by the football while I put the finishing touches on dinner, but often a planned activity is required after dessert is finished and the football is over. Every year I make sure I organise a few fun indoor activities, like yarn-sorting or used-giftwrap refolding, but for some reason, guests often leave suddenly once I bring out the yarn basket.

EVERYBODY OUT!

If the yarn basket doesn't scare them off, it's time to get creative. It is entirely up to you to decide when you would like your guests to vacate your home, and for me, I love to get a solid two hours of cleaning in after my final guest has left. A good trick to get the last guest off the couch and out the door so I can vacuum under the couch cushions is to ask them to assist me with my twelve-step washing-up plan (and that's just for the glassware).

CHANDLER'S GUIDE

TO SURVIVING THE CORPORATE WORLD

Chandler Bing has logged his fair share of hours in the office. Although it is never really clear exactly what Chandler actually does, over the course of ten seasons, Chandler upgrades his entry-level cubicle for the coveted corner office, followed by a departure to advertising in later seasons to follow his dream. As a result, there is nobody more qualified to guide you through surviving the corporate landscape than Chandler Bing. So forget about the W.E.N.U.S. (Weekly Estimated Net Usage Statistic) and don't even consider that A.N.U.S (Annual Net Usage Statistic) – just sit down and take note of Chandler's savvy guide to navigating the corporate jungle.

ARRIVING AT WORK

I like to arrive at work with as little fanfare as possible, as this avoids drawing any attention that could lead to a thirty-minute conversation about what Steve from Accounts thought of last night's episode of *Survivor*. My preferred mode of stealth is to exit the lifts a floor below mine, take the stairwell to my floor and cut a path to my desk via the stationery room. This tactic also ensures early access to the best pens.

SMALL TALK

It seems like a large proportion of my workday is taken up with inane small talk. If your colleagues love to talk, you can always just feign interest in David's golf weekend or Betty's curtain rod mix-up while you plan your escape. The only scenario worse than too much office chatter is the awkward pause in conversation, often found within those moments of forced socialisation at work events. If the burden of starting a conversation lies with you, you're going to need an arsenal of foolproof small-talk topics to survive. I usually start with the weather, move into sports, and then start describing in detail my aunt's foot surgery until everyone walks away.

AVOIDING MEETINGS

You must always, *always* appear to be busier than you are, if only to avoid the worst thing about any job, and that is attending meetings. Simulating work can be achieved in a number of ways, and if your computer screen faces away from your colleagues, even better. There is nothing more convincing than my 'busy' face, usually reserved for my most important fantasy football planning.

THE DREADED OFFICE PARTY

Could office parties *be* any more painful? I normally avoid these like the plague, but occasionally I have to attend just to fit in. They say you should never drink at office parties, and this is for good reason – you don't want to be the guy who has one too many beers and tells the boss what they really think of the team restructure – or worse, waking up the next morning to remember that you made out with Jane from Payroll, who also happens to still be asleep next to you in bed. My standard rule for these occasions is to drink nothing, fill up on snacks and ghost the party as early as humanly possible.

Chandler entered a Vanilla Ice lookalike contest and WON!

Ross came fourth
and CRIED!

THE BEST OF
FRIENDS

TOP 10 EPISODES

While I can highly recommend starting at the first episode
and bingeing all ten seasons until finished, if you're pressed for time
and just want to relive the highlights, here's a guide to the best
Friends episodes of all time.

SEASON 2, EPISODE 14
'THE ONE WITH THE PROM VIDEO'

The 1980s flashback episodes of *Friends* have always been audience favourites, and none more so than this one. This episode follows up on an earlier storyline where Ross has broken up with Julie to be with Rachel, but Rachel finds the insulting list Ross has used to decide which woman he will choose. Justifiably devastated, Rachel calls it off.

The episode begins with Ross lamenting that Rachel will probably start dating other guys. Phoebe consoles him with the lobster story – that lobsters mate for life, and that Rachel is Ross' 'lobster'. Ross makes a bad attempt at relaying this to Rachel at Central Perk, and she makes it clear that they can never be together.

Meanwhile, Monica's parents visit with a box of old keepsakes from her teenage years. Amongst the boxes, Monica finds an old home video of her and Rachel's prom night, which everyone decides to watch – except Ross, who hesitates. From the video we learn that when Rachel believes she has been stood up by her prom date, Ross' parents convince him to take her instead. Just as he walks down the stairs, we see Rachel and her date leaving for prom. This is news to Rachel, who never knew about Ross' gesture. The episode concludes with one of *Friends'* most romantic moments, as Ross and Rachel kiss and are finally an item.

He's her lobster!

43

SEASON 2, EPISODE 15:
'THE ONE WHERE ROSS AND RACHEL ...
YOU KNOW'

The title of this episode pretty much speaks for itself. Yes, this is the one with Ross and Rachel's first date, followed by their slightly more successful second date. After dinner plans go awry thanks to Ross being called into the museum, Ross has a solution. He leads Rachel to the Planetarium, where they *scene missing* under the stars to the soothing sounds of Chris Isaak. Ah, so romantic, so 90s.

This episode is also when we first meet ophthalmologist Richard Burke, a friend of Ross and Monica's parents. After Monica caters a party for Richard, she denies having a crush on him to Phoebe, but is clearly besotted. At her eye appointment later that week, one thing leads to another and they kiss. This leads to a date, where they both have second thoughts over their twenty-one-year age gap. Just as the evening looks like it's over, they kiss again. So much new romance in one episode! Awwwww.

Oh, come on, would you just grab my ass?!

SEASON 3, EPISODE 1:
'THE ONE WITH THE PRINCESS LEIA FANTASY'

Richard and Monica have just broken up, and much to Joey's disappointment, Chandler is dating Janice again. Janice decides she is going to make Joey love her, and plans 'Janice and Joey's Day of Fun'. Needless to say, it does not work! Meanwhile, Ross and Chandler have a conversation about their bedroom fantasies. Chandler admits to sometimes having fantasies that are interrupted by images of his own mother. Horrified, Ross totally judges Chandler, only to find the Princess Leia fantasy that Rachel indulges him in being interrupted by images of his own mother. Ouch!

This episode truly encapsulates how we all feel after a devastating breakup. Monica is a mess. She's unable to sleep, cries all day and grieves over one of Richard's cigar butts she found on the balcony. In a delightful daddy–daughter moment, Jack calls by the apartment to check on Monica. He finds her dishevelled on the couch,

smoking a cigar and watching Richard's Civil War videos. Finally, Jack tells Monica exactly what she needs to hear – that Richard is a mess too, and is taking their breakup harder than his earlier divorce. With this news, Monica finally falls asleep, and our hearts break just a tiny bit.

This guy is so stupid. It's COUNT RUSHMORE!

SEASON 3, EPISODE 6:
'THE ONE WITH THE FLASHBACK'

Another flashback episode, this time initiated by Janice asking if any of the Friends have ever slept together. The flashbacks take us back to a time a year before Rachel's planned wedding with Barry, when Central Perk is still a bar and Ross is still married to Carol.

Phoebe has been living with Monica but it isn't working out. Phoebe decides to move back to her grandmother's apartment, but keeps it a secret from Monica by moving one household item at a time. Meanwhile, Chandler is living across the hall and is in the market for a new roommate too. Joey applies for the room, and Chandler invites him to move in. Monica introduces herself to Joey in the hall, which Joey misinterprets as Monica hitting on him. When she invites him in for a soda, he takes off all his clothes in anticipation. Monica is shocked and drops her glass, and Joey is mortified.

Perhaps the most unexpected twist is that Rachel nearly sleeps with Chandler... you heard right! Rachel is still engaged to Barry, and visits the bar that is soon to be Central Perk. Chandler overhears Rachel talking about how she'd love to have one final fling before getting married, and basically falls over himself to talk to her. Later in

the episode, we see Rachel approach Chandler after the bar is closed and they begin to make out. Just as our jaws hit the floor, we realise that it's simply a daydream of Rachel's as she returns home in a cab.

If the Chandler/Rachel hook-up sounds unlikely, the Ross/Phoebe hook-up after Ross finds out Carol is a lesbian is equally perplexing. Their make-out moment on the bar's pool table is short-lived when they realise they are being crazy, just moments before their friends walk in. The episode ends with Chandler and Monica sharing a sweet and slightly prophetic moment when Chandler consoles Monica for not having a boyfriend.

Cute Naked Guy is really starting to put on weight.

SEASON 3, EPISODE 8:
'THE ONE WITH THE GIANT POKING DEVICE'

Phoebe breaks a tooth, but refuses to go to the dentist because every time she sees a dentist, somebody dies. After much convincing, Phoebe reluctantly gets treated, and after calling everyone she knows, thinks she may have broken the curse. Everything appears to be fine until it looks like Ugly Naked Guy isn't moving around so much anymore. The gang construct a giant poking device out of chopsticks, and their fears are allayed when Ugly Naked Guy wakes up and lives to be naked another day.

Meanwhile, Chandler and Janice have reconnected, and it seems Chandler is finally capable of falling in love. But there's one big problem: Joey sees Janice kissing her ex-husband and father of her child, the Mattress King himself. Joey agonises over telling Chandler because he doesn't want to hurt him, but ends up telling him when it looks like Chandler is going to buy Janice an expensive gift.

Chandler confronts Janice and she admits to the affair, but she is conflicted – she loves both Chandler and her ex. Joey tries to convince Chandler to step aside because Janice has a baby with her ex, and it looks

like he might, but when it comes to letting her go, Janice ends up having to be strong and makes the decision for Chandler.

Chandler tries to stop Janice from leaving by stealing her shoe, but she limps out of Central Perk and out of Chandler's life (for a while, anyway). The episode ends with Chandler tearfully hugging a Lionel Richie record and listening to 'Endless Love'. Janice is gone, but we finally see Chandler's vulnerable side. Oh Chandler, we knew you had it in you!

If the Homo sapiens were, in fact, 'homo', is that why they went extinct?'

SEASON 3, EPISODE 25:
'THE ONE AT THE BEACH'

A pivotal episode for Ross and Rachel fans, this episode takes the Friends on a trip to the beach. Phoebe is in search of her birth mother, and the gang accompany her on a holiday to the town where her mother's friend (also called Phoebe) lives so she can find out more about her mom. Meanwhile, Ross is dating Bonnie, an old friend of Phoebe's, and surprise surprise – Rachel isn't happy about it. Rachel is thrilled that Bonnie can't make it on the trip, and starts flirting with Ross at the first opportunity.

Phoebe surprises her mom's friend, and they have a happy but slightly awkward conversation. Phoebe senses that her mom's friend might be hiding something from her, so Phoebe takes matters into her own hands and returns later to snoop around the house. She gets caught, and her mom's friend admits that she isn't a friend after all – she is actually Phoebe's birth mother.

Meanwhile, back at the beach house, the tension between Ross and Rachel is palpable, but it all gets derailed by Bonnie surprising them with her arrival just as the 'Strip *Happy Days*' game is heating up. Later, Rachel convinces Bonnie that she looked better with no hair (Bonnie used to shave her head) – and much to Ross' horror, Bonnie shaves it all off.

Ross confronts Rachel about what she did, and Rachel admits she still loves him. They kiss for a moment, but Rachel tells Ross he must choose between them. The episode ends with Ross standing between Rachel and Bonnie's bedrooms. This is a season-ending cliff-hanger, so you'll have to watch episode one of season four to find out what happened...

> *Yeah, well, I couldn't find any cards, so it was either this or Strip Bag-of-old-knitting-stuff.*

SEASON 4, EPISODE 6:
'THE ONE WITH THE DIRTY GIRL'

This episode is a classic for two reasons. Firstly, Chandler realises he is falling for Joey's girlfriend Cathy, and it is heartbreaking and hilarious. Secondly, Ross is dating a beautiful palaeontologist who turns out to be the messiest woman who ever lived, and their apartment make-out session is one of the funniest moments ever.

Chandler buys Cathy a first edition of her favourite book, *The Velveteen Rabbit*. When he realises that giving her the book would make his feelings too obvious, he gallantly gives Joey the book to give to Cathy. Later, Cathy gets Chandler alone and thanks him for choosing the book because SHE KNOWS. They have 'a moment' and we all cry for Chandler.

Meanwhile, Ross is dating Cheryl, a colleague from the museum. Cheryl is smart, beautiful and loves dinosaurs as much as Ross, but there is a problem: Cheryl lives in the messiest apartment that has ever existed. Horrified, Ross realises he'll have to make peace with Cheryl's apocalyptic apartment if they're going to be together. In a hilarious scene, Ross and Cheryl begin making out on her couch. As he makes his move, his hand slips behind a cushion and straight into a piece of luncheon meat. Taking it in his stride, Ross appears to be getting over the mess – until he attacks a stray rodent wandering across the room inside a bag of potato chips. Cheryl panics and thinks it's Mitsi the hamster, but no – it's just a giant rat. Monica gets wind of Cheryl's apartment and turns up unannounced to clean it, and Ross finds himself single again.

> *Well, like that, only that instead of a chair it's a pile of garbage. And instead of a jacket it's a pile of garbage. And instead of the end of the day it's the end of time, and garbage is all that has survived.'*

SEASON 5, EPISODE 11:
'THE ONE WITH ALL THE RESOLUTIONS'

It's New Year's Eve, and the gang all make New Year's resolutions. Chandler decides to stop making fun of people; Phoebe wants to learn how to fly a plane; Joey decides to learn guitarp; and Monica will take up photography. Pivotal to the plot of this episode is Ross resolving to try something new every day, and Rachel pledging to stop gossiping.

Walking past a leather store, Ross decides to buy a pair of leather pants because he's 'never had a nice-smelling pair of pants before'. Ross wears them on a date with Elizabeth, and it soon becomes obvious that they weren't such a great idea when he starts to overheat, and the sweaty pants make some unflattering noises against the couch. Hot and bothered, Ross retreats to the bathroom and splashes water against his legs for some relief. As he goes to pull the pants back up, he realises they are stuck.

Freaking out, Ross calls Joey for some advice. Unfortunately Joey's advice is to add some baby powder to the mix, followed by some lotion... but all this does is create a giant sticky mess. When Elizabeth finally discovers what Ross has

been up to in the bathroom, you guessed it – Ross finds himself single again.

Meanwhile, this is the episode where Rachel finds out about Chandler and Monica. Rachel picks up the phone to make a call and overhears a raunchy conversation that Monica is having. Intrigued, Rachel listens in, but is shocked to discover it's Chandler that Monica is flirting with. Even though she is forbidden to gossip, Rachel confides in Joey that she knows about Chandler and Monica.

Which leads us to the next episode – one that, in this author's humble opinion, is the greatest *Friends* episode of all time...

> *I'm gonna go out on a limb and say, 'No divorces in '99.' Whoo.'*

SEASON 5, EPISODE 14:
'THE ONE WHERE EVERYBODY FINDS OUT'

Chandler and Monica have been sneaking around together for months. Joey knows, Rachel knows, but Phoebe and Ross do not. Ugly Naked Guy is moving out of his apartment, and Ross decides to apply for it. When inspecting the apartment, Phoebe looks into Monica's apartment and sees Monica and Chandler getting busy.

Phoebe is shocked, and Rachel has to calm her down so Ross doesn't find out. Rachel and Phoebe decide to have a little fun with Monica and Chandler. Phoebe decides to start flirting outrageously with Chandler at Central Perk. Later, when Chandler tells Monica that Phoebe was hitting on him, Monica puts two and two together and realises that Phoebe must know their secret and is trying to freak them out.

Chandler and Monica decide to retaliate, and the 'messers become the messees', with Joey stuck in the middle. When Phoebe suggests meeting Chandler later in his apartment, and Chandler agrees, Phoebe and Rachel realise that 'they don't know that we know they know we know'. Phoebe turns up for the date: cue hilarity!

As they psych each other out with the proposition of taking things to the bedroom, Chandler finally freaks out and admits he's in love with Monica. Monica overhears this and is thrilled, and Joey is thrilled their secret is finally out. Unfortunately for Joey, Monica and Chandler decide to keep things a secret from Ross for the time being. This idea backfires the next day when Ross is in his new apartment and sees the same thing Phoebe saw through the window. At least everyone knows now!

I'm very bendy.

SEASON 6, EPISODE 10:
'THE ONE WITH THE ROUTINE'

It is the lead-up to Christmas, and Joey has fallen hard for his beautiful new roommate Janine (played by supermodel Elle Macpherson). Janine is a professional dancer and has been hired to be a background dancer for Dick Clark's *New Year's Rockin' Eve*. Janine asks Joey if he'd like to be a background dancer too, and he jumps at the chance to spend more time with her.

We all love Joey (Janine – not so much!), but the highlight of this episode is definitely Ross and Monica's incredibly hilarious dancing. Despite their smooth moves, Ross and Monica want to dance on the podium, but keep getting overlooked. The less they get noticed by the director, the harder they dance, but to no avail. Finally,

Ross suggests bringing out the big guns – a dance routine they used to rehearse in middle school and once won them an honourable mention in the brother/sister dance category.

Ross and Monica dance their booties off, but the filming ends before they get their chance at TV stardom. Similarly, Joey's chance to kiss Janine at 'fake midnight' is cut short, but they end up kissing for real later that night back at the apartment. Joey and Janine's relationship turns out to be short-lived, but 'the routine' by Ross and Monica will echo through the ages.

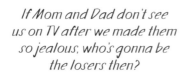

If Mom and Dad don't see us on TV after we made them so jealous, who's gonna be the losers then?

You were under the pile of COATS?

I WAS the pile of coats!

OH. MY. GOD.

JANICE: EVERYONE'S FAVOURITE EX-GIRLFRIEND

Janice Litman-Goralnik (née Hosenstein) is one of *Friends*' most beloved recurring characters, and in this author's opinion, has the best wardrobe of all the cast. From her first appearance, Janice has a knack for turning up in Chandler's life at exactly the wrong time, always with hilarious results.

We first meet Janice when Chandler enlists Phoebe to help him break up with her, because he doesn't trust himself to follow through with it. This tactic clearly doesn't work, with Janice and Chandler having an on-again-off-again relationship for the next four seasons.

Even after Chandler and Monica become an item, Janice still turns up in Chandler's life from time to time. Of course Janice uses the same fertility clinic as Chandler and Monica, and when they decide to buy a house in the suburbs, Janice is considering buying the house next door. Perhaps the greatest Janice moment was when she turns up in the birthing suite next to Rachel and Ross when Emma is born. Oh. My. God. Indeed!

What's so great about Janice is that she has heart. Let's face it – Janice brought out the best in Chandler before he found love with Monica. Who could forget the first time Chandler had loved and lost Janice, and we see him tearfully cradling a Lionel Richie album while listening to 'Endless Love'?

Janice is played by the talented Maggie Wheeler, who portrayed Janice across thirteen hilarious episodes. While Wheeler is best known for her role as Janice, she has appeared in dozens of TV shows, including *L.A. Law*, *Ellen*, *Will & Grace* and *Seinfeld*, playing a character who momentarily believes she has been impregnated by none other than George Costanza.

55

THE ONE WHERE PHOEBE MARRIES THE PERFECT MAN, MIKE HANNIGAN

Go on, admit it – we're all a bit in love with Mike Hannigan. Mike was portrayed by everyone's favourite ageless Hollywood heart-throb, Paul Rudd. It was no doubt a big ask for any comedic actor to become an honorary Friend by marrying into the group, but Rudd absolutely nailed the role and became an audience favourite across seventeen episodes during the final two seasons.

Mike charmed us from his first appearance in 'The One with the Paediatrician', where Joey and Phoebe decide to go on a double blind date. When Joey forgets to organise a date for Phoebe, he lies and tells her that his friend Mike will be her date. Joey simply shouts the name Mike until he finds one in Central Perk – enter Mike Hannigan.

Mike used to be a lawyer, but gave it all up to become a professional pianist. Mike and Phoebe instantly hit it off, and everything is going well until Phoebe finds out that after his earlier divorce, Mike never wants to get married again. Not convinced that the relationship can go anywhere, Phoebe calls it off with Mike, and ends up getting back together with David.

The writers of *Friends* had originally planned for this to be the end of Mike and Phoebe, and for Phoebe to marry David; however, audiences adored Mike, and the writers decided they should end up together instead. While David was great, we were all thrilled when Phoebe and Mike finally tied the knot – knowing once and for all that love is real. Awwwww!

It bodes well
for me that speed
impresses you.

PAGING DR BURKE,
THE WORLD'S SEXIEST OPHTHALMOLOGIST

Dr Richard Burke walked into our lives and stole our hearts at the end of season two. Audiences swooned over the significantly older Richard, a friend of Ross and Monica's parents, who Monica reconnects with when catering a party for him.

It's immediately clear that Monica and Richard are attracted to each other, and Monica books an eye appointment with Richard as an excuse to see him again. They end up kissing, which leads to a date where Monica has second thoughts upon realising that Richard is a grandfather. Just as Richard goes to leave, they kiss again, and thus begins one of the great love affairs on *Friends*.

Monica and Richard are crazy for each other, but the age gap proves too vast when Monica mentions wanting to start a family together one day. Richard loves Monica, but he already has grown children from his first marriage and doesn't want

to start all over again. We all died a little inside when Richard and Monica broke up at Barry and Mindy's wedding, and we've all been Monica when she runs into Richard at the video store in a pair of old sweats with panties stuck to her leg.

Richard was portrayed by Tom Selleck, a man once voted the Sexiest Man Alive by the *Ladies' Home Journal* thanks to his most famous role as Thomas Magnum in *Magnum, P.I.* The age difference between Monica and Richard on *Friends* was twenty-one years, but their chemistry was amazing – and much as we all love Chandler, Richard holds a special place in our hearts.

A TRIBUTE TO

UGLY NAKED GUY

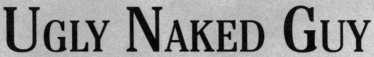

Ugly Naked Guy, we hardly knew you. In fact, we never even saw you, which is probably for the best because you were always naked, and from all accounts, it wasn't pretty.

Ugly Naked Guy lived in the apartment across from Monica and Rachel, and his 'alternative lifestyle choice' shocked and entertained the gang for many years. Who could forget classic moments like, 'Ugly Naked Guy is decorating his Christmas tree. Wow, you should see the size of his Christmas balls!' and, 'Oh look, Ugly Naked Guy is lighting candles! Ooooh! That had to hurt!'

In one episode, Phoebe is convinced that Ugly Naked Guy is dead because he isn't moving so much. The gang decides the best course of action is to poke Ugly Naked Guy to see if he is alive, and fashion a long poking device out of many pairs of chopsticks. Luckily, Ugly Naked Guy awakens, and ends up showing them his own poking device (eww).

Perhaps the most famous Ugly Naked Guy moment was in his final appearance. Ugly Naked Guy is moving out of his building, and decides to sublet his apartment. Ross decides to go for it, but competition is fierce. When Ross realises his sad gift of a small muffin basket isn't going to cut it, he turns up at Ugly Naked Guy's apartment and decides to get naked too (in a purely platonic sense, of course). Naked Ross is ultimately successful, and Ugly Naked Guy's apartment becomes Ross' apartment for the rest of the series.

63

A SERVE OF

GUNTHER'S CENTRAL PERK

You know what they say – if you think your friendship group doesn't have a Gunther, *you* are the Gunther. Never a leading man on *Friends*, Gunther was usually relegated to the background, faithfully serving the clientele of Central Perk their coffees while quietly lusting after Rachel.

Gunther has seen it all: from Rachel and Ross' first breakup over the 'copy girl', right through to declaring his undying love for Rachel before she flies to Paris in the final episode, 'Just in case that changes things for you.'

Want to recreate Gunther's Central Perk hospitality at home? Here are three recipes sure to impress.

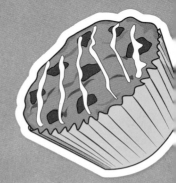

BLUEBERRY COCONUT MUFFINS

375 g (2½ cups) plain (all-purpose) flour
2 teaspoons baking powder
150 g (⅔ cup) brown sugar
150 g (1 cup) blueberries, fresh or frozen
1 egg
250 ml (1 cup) whole milk
50 ml (1¾ fl oz) vegetable oil
65 g (1 cup) shredded coconut

Preheat the oven to 200°C (400°F), or 180°C (350°F) if fan-forced. Line a 12-hole muffin tin with paper cases.

Sift the flour and baking powder into a mixing bowl. Stir in the sugar and gently fold in the blueberries.

In a separate bowl, beat together the egg, milk and oil. Add to the dry ingredients and mix until just combined.

Spoon the mixture into the muffin tin, then sprinkle each muffin with the coconut.

Bake for 20 minutes, or until the muffins have risen and a skewer inserted in the comes out clean.

OAT & RAISIN COOKIES

220 g (8 oz) unsalted butter, at room temperature
150 g (¾ cup lightly packed) brown sugar
150 g (¾ cup) caster (superfine) sugar
2 eggs
1 teaspoon natural vanilla extract
225 g (1½ cups) plain (all-purpose) flour
1 teaspoon baking powder
285 g (3 cups) rolled oats
130 g (¾ cup) raisins

Preheat the oven to 180°C (350°F), or 160°C (315°F) if fan-forced. Line two baking trays with baking paper.

In a large bowl, cream the butter, brown sugar and caster sugar until pale. Add the eggs and vanilla extract, mixing well until combined.

Sift the flour and baking powder into the bowl, then stir in the oats and raisins.

Roll spoonfuls of the batter into about 30 balls, then place each one on the baking trays with enough space for them to expand. Flatten each one slightly, using a fork.

Bake for 12–15 minutes, or until lightly golden in colour. Cool on the tray for 10 minutes, before transferring to a wire rack to cool completely.

GUNTHER'S ULTIMATE
HOT CHOCOLATE FOR TWO

50 g (1¾ oz) high-quality dark or milk chocolate
500 ml (2 cups) whole milk
marshmallows, to serve

Gently melt the chocolate using a double boiler, or in a small saucepan suspended over a larger saucepan of boiling water. Stir until melted, being very careful not to splash any water into the chocolate.

Once melted, pour the chocolate into two large coffee mugs.

Gently heat the milk in a small saucepan until hot but not boiling. Carefully pour the milk into both mugs, stirring to combine.

Top each mug with marshmallows and serve.

TIP: For an extra-special touch, gently blowtorch the marshmallows until lightly browned before serving.

Man this is weird. You *ever realise* Captain Crunch's eyebrows are actually on his hat?

You think THAT'S what's weird? Joey, the man's been captain of a cereal for the last forty years!

LIVING WITH YOUR

BEST FRIEND

Living with a friend can be a great experience. Or it can be a living nightmare from start to finish, leaving you begging for mercy. Nearly all of the Friends have lived together at one time or another, so who better to provide sensible advice on living with your best friend than Ross, Rachel, Monica, Chandler, Joey and Phoebe?

I just loved living with Rachel. We would just talk and laugh, and I really felt like we were on the same page on just about everything. It was so easy-going and fun. My tip for living with your best friend would be to keep things breezy.

Breezy? I once hid in the bathroom for five hours after spilling a plate of crumbs between the couch cushions moments after Monica had just finished her second tidy of the day.

Well at least PHOEBE loved living with me. Phoebe! Back me up!

I used to sleep at work on Friday nights to avoid Monica's Saturday morning spring cleans that, although clearly named after a single season, run fifty-two weeks of the year. So I guess my advice would be to recognise the best moments to make yourself scarce and avoid conflict.

Well, I've never experienced conflict with my roommates. Even though my time spent living with Chandler and Joey was short, I treasured my time in their apartment. It was so much fun just hanging out with the guys.

Yeah, we sure had some good times shooting the breeze around your air purifier.

Hey! I need that thing for my allergies! And I bet your houseplants weren't complaining.

There were no houseplants, Ross – we could barely sustain our own lives in that apartment.

Joey and I had a great arrangement when it was just the two of us. We could hang out for hours in the recliners watching endless episodes of BAYWATCH, but we knew how to give each other space. I remember when I used to bring women home and Joey would just know to make himself scarce.

Dude, that happened, like, twice in five years.

Maybe I was too emotionally scarred to bring home women after listening to you entertain your house guests through our paper-thin walls. Tip for living with someone like Joey: industrial earplugs may not be enough.

I guess it's just Phoebe and I who haven't lived together yet.

Oh we've lived together, Joey. Just not in this life.

SON OF A BING!

WHO IS CHARLES BING?

We first meet Charles Bing in Las Vegas, starring as Helena Handbasket in his cabaret show *Viva Las Gaygas* at the Four Queens Casino. Monica and Chandler decide to visit Charles after Monica insists Chandler patch things up with his estranged father before their wedding day.

It turns out that Chandler and Charles haven't spoken for years. We never find out why, but perhaps Chandler still harboured bad feelings after Charles and his mother told him they were getting a divorce when he was nine years old – at Thanksgiving Dinner. Or maybe when Charles ran off with Chandler's gym teacher Mr Garibaldi. I guess we'll never know.

During the cabaret show, Charles and Chandler patch things up, and Chandler invites his father to the wedding. Moments later, Charles breaks into song with 'It's Raining Men', with Chandler regretfully informing Monica that he used to be the dancer on the right.

Charles was played by Kathleen Turner for four episodes of *Friends*. While audiences were delighted at the time, the role of Charles has dated since the episode aired, and Turner has reportedly stated that she doesn't think the show has 'aged well'.

Pivot!
Pivot!
Pivot!

Shut up!
Shut up!
Shut up!

77

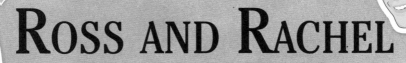

ROSS AND RACHEL

RELATIONSHIP TIMELINE

FIRST MET

Ross and Rachel first met back in high school. Rachel was Monica's best friend, and Ross loved Rachel from afar... for the next ten years.

FIRST MOMENT

Rachel and Ross' first romantic moment was at Rachel and Monica's prom night, though Rachel didn't learn of this until years later. When Rachel's date doesn't turn up, Ross puts on a suit and prepares to take her – but then Rachel's date turns up and Ross' plans are derailed, to his great disappointment. However, this tender moment was captured in Monica's prom video.

I mean, I didn't even get to tell you that I love you too. Because of course I do. I love you. I love you. I love you.

FIRST KISS

Ross and Rachel's first kiss was at Central Perk, after Ross finds out that Rachel has feelings for him thanks to the drunken phone message she left on his answering machine the night before. Ross confronts Rachel as she is closing the coffee shop, and they initially have an argument. As Rachel cries on the couch, Ross knocks at the door. She lets him in, and they share their first kiss.

FIRST DATE

Ross is supposed to take Rachel to dinner, but at the last minute gets called into the museum to work. Rachel accompanies him, and just when it looks like the evening is over, Ross surprises her with dinner from a vending machine under the stars in the museum's planetarium.

> *You're over me? When were you ... under me?*

FIRST BREAKUP

We were on a break! Or at least this is what Ross was thinking when Rachel tells him they need to take a break from each other after he becomes jealous of her relationship with her colleague Mark. Ross ends up drunkenly sleeping with a girl from the copy place, and when Rachel finds out, it is all over.

> We were on a break!

> I got off the plane.

MOST MEMORABLE MOMENT

There have been many enduring Ross and Rachel moments, but perhaps the most unforgettable was in the final episode of *Friends*, when they finally get back together for good. Rachel is about to board a plane for Paris when Ross confronts her at the airport and begs her not to go. Ross is devastated when she gets on the plane… but when he returns home, he hears Rachel's message on his answering machine professing her love – just like old times! Moments later she knocks at the door, and we know Ross and Rachel are back together forever.

CHANDLER AND MONICA

RELATIONSHIP TIMELINE

FIRST MET

Chandler was Ross' college roommate, so Monica met Chandler while she was still in high school. In a flashback episode, we find out that Chandler actually dissed Monica about her weight when they were in college, and that's what spurred her on to get thin. That's right – Monica 'revenge bodied' Chandler. Lucky he grew up into a nice guy, because that was totally not okay!

CHANDLER

MONICA

FIRST MOMENT

Chandler and Monica had a few special moments before their fling in London, though none of us expected their future romance. In a touching scene, Chandler comforts Monica about not having a boyfriend. Chandler tells her she's the most beautiful woman he's ever met in real life, and as they hug, he says, 'This feels good.' Of course, he's talking about the towel she's wearing, but it's a sweet moment nonetheless.

You make me happier than I ever thought I could be. And if you'll let me, I will spend the rest of my life trying to make you feel the same way.

FIRST KISS

The gang are in London for Ross and Emily's wedding, and Monica is feeling low after being mistaken for Ross' mother at the rehearsal dinner. She seeks comfort from Chandler, and they end up in bed together. Their first kiss certainly coincided with another big 'first' for the couple as well!

> Get off my sister!

FIRST DATE

Monica and Chandler don't really have an official first date, considering they ran around in secret for months after returning from London. Let's say their first date was within the first few minutes of arriving home to New York, while still on 'London time', and leave it at that...

FIRST BREAKUP

While not officially a breakup, Chandler gets cold feet right before their wedding. He is worried that he and Monica will end up unhappy like his parents, and escapes to his office. Fortunately he is found by Ross, who talks him off the ledge.

> Look, we're not just messing around! I love her. Okay, I'm in love with her.

You're a really good kisser!

MOST MEMORABLE MOMENT

Monica and Chandler's incredibly romantic proposal scene is one of the best *Friends* moments of all time. After an earlier false start thanks to Chandler being a fool and Richard Burke turning up and nearly ruining everything, Monica realises Chandler is the one. When Chandler turns up at the apartment to propose, it is filled with candles. Monica gets down on one knee, then Chandler gets on one knee too, and everything is the best ever! Monica says yes, and the rest is history.

GETTING OVER
A BREAKUP

The Friends have all had their fair share of heartbreak over the years. We all felt it when Monica cried on the couch watching Civil War documentaries and smoking cigars to remind herself of Richard – and who can forget Phoebe saying goodbye to David when he moved to Minsk to follow his dream of finally completing the positronic distillation of subatomic particles? When you need help mending a broken heart, the Friends are here to help you.

Civil War
1861

My best tip to get over heartbreak is to keep yourself distracted and busy with fun projects. This is the perfect opportunity to clean your house from top to bottom, sort through your sock drawer, and dust between and underneath each individual book in your bookcase.

Self-care is so important after a breakup. Give yourself the time and space to look after yourself and get your priorities in order. Priorities like which department store to hit first, and which credit card you'll take to each store.

I certainly found having an ocean and 3500 miles between me and Emily to be the best possible solution to accidentally dropping another woman's name at the altar. For me, the easiest way to get over a breakup is to start working on the next.

I find the only way to move on is to get back out there as soon as humanly possible. The longer you linger over what could have been, the longer it takes to feel better. It used to take me up to forty-eight hours to get over a breakup, but years of experience have whittled that down to about two hours.

I would have to say that the 'scorched earth' technique is the best way to deal with exes. Don't call, don't text and stop following them on social media. You should go to great lengths to avoid running into them – possibly moving cities if necessary.

After a breakup, I like to really throw myself into creative projects. I either write a new song, work on a new painting, or create a voodoo doll of my ex made of whatever clothing and nail-clippings he left at my house.

Oh, sorry.
Did I get you?

NO, you didn't get me. It's an electric DRILL. You get me, you KILL me!

BEST FRIENDS

FOREVER!

Think you know your Friends? Okay, this is it: fifteen
questions to separate the *Friends* noobs from the *Friends*
know-it-alls. So sit down, pour yourself a cappuccino in an
oversized 90s receptacle and put your thinking cap on –
it's time to take the ultimate trivia test!

1. What was the brand of Japanese men's lipstick that Joey advertised? *Ubani? Chibani*

2. According to Rachel, what is Chandler's occupation?

3. What is the stage name of Chandler's father?

4. What was the name of Monica's childhood Easy-Bake Oven restaurant?

5. Which entire US band is in Phoebe's little black book?

6. Which dinosaur does Ross hypothesise made a high-pitched, intimidating noise to threaten predators? *pterydactly*

7. How many sisters does Joey have? *7*

8. What are the names of Frank Jr.'s triplets that Phoebe gave birth to?
   Leslie, Chandler, Frank Jr Jr

9. What did Ross say that Rachel's Thanksgiving trifle tasted like? *Feet*

10. What is the fake name that Phoebe often provides? *Regina Phalange*

11. What was the name of the play Joey starred in that convinced Estelle to become his manager? *Mac & Cheese?*

12. What did Ross and Monica's nanna keep stashed in her wardrobe? *Sweet & low*

13. During the New York blackout, the gang discuss the craziest place they have ever 'done it'. What is Rachel's answer? *guys parents bed*

14. Name three of the adult films that Ursula starred in using Phoebe's name.

15. Who was Monica's first kiss with?

ANSWERS

1. Ichiban Lipstick For Men **2.** Transponster **3.** Helena Handbasket
4. Easy Monica's Bakery **5.** Jethro Tull **6.** Velociraptor **7.** Seven **8.** Frank Jr. Jr.,
Leslie and Chandler **9.** Feet **10.** Regina Phalange **11.** *Freud! The Musical*
12. Sweet'N Low **13.** The foot of the bed **14.** Any three of the following:
*Lawrence of a Labia, Inspect Her Gadget, Sex Toy Story 2, Buffay the
Vampire Layer* **15.** Ross! (Don't freak out – it was in a darkened college
bedroom, and Ross thought she was Rachel)

WHAT KIND OF
FRIEND ARE YOU?

0–5: *Friends* noob

Someone clearly bought you this gift as a Secret Santa but you've never seen an episode. My advice to you is to start watching *Friends* immediately.

5–10: Entry-level *Friends* fan

You have a decent knowledge of the show, but maybe only watched the final seasons once or twice. SHAME ON YOU.

14–15: *Friends* expert

Are you the couch from Central Perk? Because it seems like you've heard everything ever said during all ten seasons of *Friends*. You are truly a *Friends* expert, and I doff my cap to you!

11–13: *Friends* aficionado

You have seen every episode multiple times, but you may wish to consider purchasing further copies of this book to leave around your house so that you can really become an expert. Watching five episodes a day wouldn't go astray either.

I got her machine.

Her answering machine?

No, interestingly enough her leafblower picked up.

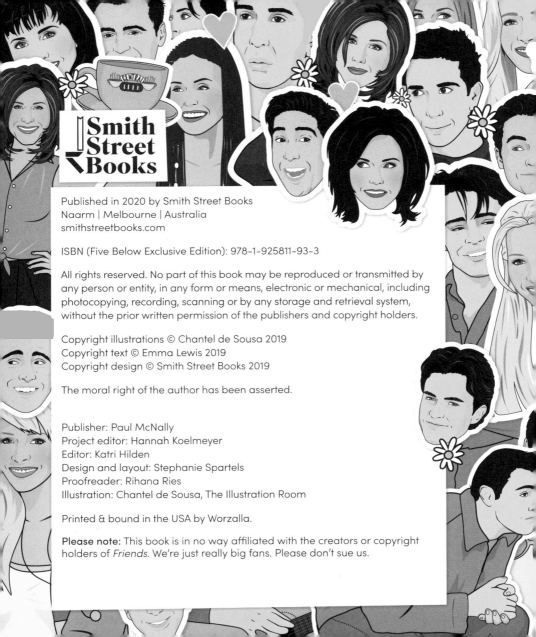

Published in 2020 by Smith Street Books
Naarm | Melbourne | Australia
smithstreetbooks.com

ISBN (Five Below Exclusive Edition): 978-1-925811-93-3

Publisher: Paul McNally
Project editor: Hannah Koelmeyer
Editor: Katri Hilden
Design and layout: Stephanie Spartels
Proofreader: Rihana Ries
Illustration: Chantel de Sousa, The Illustration Room

Printed & bound in the USA by Worzalla.

Please note: This book is in no way affiliated with the creators or copyright holders of *Friends*. We're just really big fans. Please don't sue us.